MW01681296

UNWANTED CHANGES

BITS OF WISDOM AND HOPE FOR YOUR GRIEVING HEART

BARBARA LEE KIRCHNER

Copyright @ 2010 by Barbara Lee Kirchner

Cover photo by Richard Kirchner

Author's photo by Danielle Kirchner

All rights reserved.

No part of this publication may be reproduced, distributed, or transmitted in any form or by any means-electronic, mechanical, photocopying, recording, or otherwise-except for brief quotations in printed reviews, or stored in a database or retrieval system, without the prior written permission of the publisher.

Published by Barbara Lee Kirchner
Peaceful Moments, LLC
P.O. Box 551
Sauk Rapids, MN 56379

Barbara L. Kirchner is not a licensed counselor, therapist, psychologist or psychiatrist. The views presented in this book are based on Barbara's personal life experiences and trainings she has received in the area of grief.

ISBN 978-0-9845851-0-6

Dedicated to my beloved husband

Daniel John Kirchner
February 15, 1962 – June 4, 2002

And

Our four children: Rachelle, Brian, Ricky, and Danielle

My love for them is indescribable.
They bring joy and meaning to my life!
They are his legacy.

FOREWORD

I know everyone has a story. I am even willing to admit there are more tragic stories than mine. But, to me, because I'm living it, mine is the most tragic.

On June 4, 2002, my husband left for work and never came home again.

He was a strong and healthy man. He was only 40 years old.

My beloved husband, Dan, was killed in a work accident.

We have four children, two girls and two boys. Their ages at the time of his death were: 15, 13, 11 and 8.

CONTENTS

INTRODUCTION

Please accept my condolences for your loss. Unfortunately, there are no magical words to take your pain away. My dream is that this book will touch your heart and bring you some hope.

Today, I have hope. I have worked hard and it has been eight years since I became a widow at the age of 38.

In this book, you will find my raw emotions. The ones I felt as I was traveling through the early days, weeks, and months of my grief journey. My family and I have had to endure countless unwanted changes. Hopefully, you will notice an improvement in my feelings as I grow and change and more time passes. Scattered in between all the emotions and feelings, I share with you bits of wisdom I've acquired along the way. I pray my writings will bring you some comfort and healing.

I have deliberately kept this book short because one of the many things I've learned is while you're grieving your attention span is minimized.

Wisdom Bit #1

Make sure you are eating and sleeping ***every****day*.

Losing My Best Friend

Please don't try to "fix" this for me.

No one can.

My loved one, my best friend, is gone.

And although many well-meaning family

members and friends will say, "You'll

get over this," it is simply not true!

I may get *through* it, and time will

probably ease my pain, but I know the

pain will always be there.

I believe I will have to learn to live with it.

The support of family and friends is

priceless!!

Wisdom Bit #2

Be gentle with yourself.

Wisdom Bit #3

Lean on God.

The Children

Oh, NOOOOOO!

How do I raise the children *alone*?!

There is never a good age to lose your

dad, but they are **so** young.

They are all still minors.

My heart *bleeds* for them.

Please, God, help us!!

Wisdom Bit #4

You may find you have a noise aversion while you're grieving.

Wisdom Bit #5

"Mindless"
work/busy work,
like dishes,
laundry and house
cleaning, can act
like a
sponge to absorb
some of your
grief.

Am I Alive?

I think I'm alive,

but it doesn't feel like it.

People say there is more to "me" than just

the part of me that was a part of "we".

I *know* that a big part of me died with

you.

Will someone **please** tell me what "part"

of me is still alive?

Because, you see, I feel dead inside.

The experts say that "I'm alive" and "I will

survive".

I hope they know what they're talking

about.

Wisdom Bit #6

You *are* alive.
It's OK to
live, laugh,
and love.

Losing You

Losing you has turned my world upside
down.
I feel like someone took all the pieces of
my life, threw them up in the air, and
said, "Catch, Barb."
And I'm running around as fast as I can
trying to catch them all before they hit
the ground.

Wisdom Bit #7

Grief is hard work!

Wisdom Bit #8

Ask for help.

The Hole Inside

There is a gaping hole in my heart.

It's a pain so deep no one can see it.

I miss him terribly!

I try to stop myself from feeling the pain

because it hurts *too* much!

I'm afraid the hole inside of me will always

be there.

Wisdom Bit #9

Your loved one would want you to be happy.

When Will I Stop Crying?

I can't stop crying.

Oh sure, I can usually control the tears in public.

But, in private, I fall apart.

It's now been a year and a half since my beloved husband was unexpectedly, abruptly, torn away from us, and

I WANT HIM BACK!

This isn't fair!

This isn't right!

Will someone please tell me: When will I stop crying?

Wisdom Bit #10

Completing even simple everyday tasks, like showering, can be a major accomplishment when you are grieving.

Why Can't They Understand?

I wish so badly they could *understand*.

And yet, I know, the only way they can

ever truly understand is if it happens

to them.

That I would NEVER wish on anyone!

So why do I keep wanting them to

understand how hard this is for us?

I guess I need to "let go" and let God.

Wisdom Bit #11

Tell people what
you need.
They don't know.

Wisdom Bit #12

Do *whatever* makes you feel better. (As long as you are **not** hurting yourself or anyone else and not damaging property.)

I Don't Have the Flu

A very wise friend helped me.

She said, "When people say, 'Get over it'

or 'Aren't you over that yet?' Say to

them, 'I don't have the *flu*'."

This is not something I'm going to just

"get over".

I do believe all people mean well and

they're trying to help, they just don't

understand.

Wisdom Bit #13

Do not let *anyone* tell you "how" to grieve.

Wisdom Bit #14

Everyone grieves differently.

Like a Clown

I feel like a clown.
I put on a happy face when inside I'm crying.
The world seems unable or unwilling to deal with my sadness.
So, I cry in private and they feel better because they see and/or think that I'm fine.
They *can't* honestly think I'm not sad anymore. Can they?
Will the world ever be comfortable with people's tears?
I don't want to act like a clown anymore.

Wisdom Bit #15

Never
"should" on
yourself.

Poor Me

I want to run away.

I want this to not be true.

How can this be happening?!

I don't want to raise four kids alone!

The experts say "you can get bitter or you can get better".

I'm really *trying* to get "better".

And the kids need me more now than ever before.

Please, God, help me get better.

I really *want* to get better!

I want to stop the "poor me" pity parties I occasionally like to throw for myself.

Wisdom Bit #16

Grief is
exhausting!
Rest as often
as you can.

Lord, Please Slow Me Down

Losing my husband has made me want to
run.
I want to run from the pain.
Staying overly busy helps my "running".
When I'm running, the pain is numbed.
However, I've discovered being numb also
stops the good feelings.
I'm learning to allow the pain to come,
including at all the unexpected times.
Feeling the pain helps me get through
this.
So, some day, I'll also be capable of
feeling the good emotions again.
Lord, *please* slow me down!

Wisdom Bit #17

The passing of time, alone, does not heal. Time *and* work heal.

I Want To Hold You

People tell me it will get better.

But as I cry, I'm only getting wetter.

I know that life will never be the same.

Will I always feel this lame?

I want to hold you in my arms,

and protect you from all life's harms.

Wisdom Bit #18

It's OK to be angry. It's NOT OK to be mean.

All That's Left is the "Sad"

The shock is gone now.

The truth stares me in the face.

My beloved husband will no longer hold

me in his arms.

The numbness that protected me is

mostly gone away.

I can no longer walk around in a fog.

The world pushes me forward and my

children need me.

However, a large part of me died the

same day my husband died.

All of the flowers from the funeral have

died, and most of the plants, too.

I tried to keep the plants watered, but I

just didn't have the energy.

(Continued)

All That's Left is the "Sad"

(continued)

The rest of the world has moved on and I

am left behind to deal with my pain.

I refuse to live in denial and I don't know

if I've "accepted" this yet.

For now, it feels like all that's left is the

"sad".

Wisdom Bit #19

You can get bitter
or you can get
better.
It's easy to get
bitter.
You have to work
to get better.

Wisdom Bit #20

Find a place where you can find peace.

Figuring It Out

With the help of time and work, I am finally figuring "it" out.

I now know:

- My family and friends will never fully understand what I'm going through unless they experience a very similar loss.
- It doesn't matter how much my husband and I disagreed, we had a very deep love for each other.
- He will always be a part of my life.
- He will live forever in my heart.
- Our four children are parts of him that are very precious gifts.

(Continued)

Figuring It Out
(Continued)

- His family of origin is a link to his childhood.
- People who have experienced a loss have a choice: they can become bitter or they can get better.
- It's easy to get bitter.
- You have to work at getting better.
- If you choose to get better, you can experience remarkable growth.
- You can grow in areas where you never knew you had strengths.
- God is carrying my children and me through this tragedy.
- We (unintentionally) take our loved ones and time for granted.

(Continued)

Figuring It Out
(Continued)

- I always thought we'd have "tomorrow".
- Time is *much* more precious than gold. (However, people will take your time, but they won't take your money……well, at least, *some* people won't.)

Wisdom Bit #21

"Letting go"
does not
mean
forgetting.
You will never
forget.

Am I Done Yet?

I really thought I was "through" my grief.

I mean, it's been two years and ten months; I "should" be through it.

Right? At least that's what society tells me.

First of all, I *know* I'm never supposed to "should" on myself.

Secondly, who cares what society thinks?!

Most importantly, I confused being "through the grief" with being "done" with the grief.

You see, I like the feeling of being "done" with something and I kept asking myself, "Am I done yet?"

(Continued)

Am I Done Yet?
(Continued)

However, the reality is, I'll NEVER really
be "done" grieving my beloved husband.
Because I'll always love him, I'll always
miss him and there will always be days
I'll cry for him.
I may, someday, be able to say: my grief
is "resolved" (whatever *that* means!)
and go on with my new and very
different life.
However, my husband will be a part of me
always because he will live forever in
my heart!
Now *that's* a good feeling!

Wisdom Bit # 22

Grief is a journey.

Today

It's been six and a half years since my
beloved husband died.
I still miss him very much.
However, I am a happy, content person.
I know I'll see him again someday.
I know he's in a better place.
Losing him has made me more
appreciative of the many blessings I
have today.
He was a blessing in my life, and our four
children are blessings and parts of him
that live on.
Today, I am hopeful for a bright future!

MY WISHES

1. I wish my kids didn't have to suffer the loss of their father when they were so young.
2. I wish I hadn't lost my husband at such a young age.
3. I wish you hadn't lost your loved one.
4. I wish I could take your pain away.
5. I wish more employers understood grief.
6. I wish our culture was more conductive to healing after the death of a loved one.

(Continued)

My Wishes
(Continued)

7. I wish our society wasn't in such a hurry.
8. I wish people knew how to comfort you.
9. I wish people didn't say hurtful things.
10. I wish people knew what to do to help you.
11. I wish it didn't take so long to feel better after a loved one dies.
12. I wish death wasn't a fact of life.
13. I wish people weren't so uncomfortable with sadness and would just allow others to be sad when they need to be, and would just sit quietly

(Continued)

My Wishes
(Continued)

with them when they're sad.

14. I wish people knew more about grief.
15. I wish I could give you what you need.
16. I wish you happiness.
17. I wish you peace.

MY HOPES

1. I hope you lean on God and allow Him to help you.
2. I hope my kids live happy lives.
3. I hope you live, laugh, and love again someday.
4. I hope you don't let this loss destroy you.
5. I hope you realize that even though your family has changed, you are still a family.

(Continued)

My Hopes
(Continued)

6. I hope you work to become a better person and don't allow yourself to become bitter.
7. I hope you learn to enjoy even the smallest, simplest pleasures in life.
8. I hope you find a reason to smile every day.
9. I hope you count your blessings.
10. I hope you realize life is fragile.
11. I hope you remember there are no guarantees in life.
12. I hope you don't stay angry.
13. I hope you slow down.

(Continued)

My Hopes
(Continued)

14. I hope you forgive yourself.
15. I hope you find happiness and peace.
16. I hope this book brought you some comfort.

Order Form

___ *Unwanted Changes* Book
(Qty)

11.95 each ________

Shipping 3.00
(For up to two books.
For larger quantities,
please call for price.)

Subtotal: ________

(Minnesota residents please add 6.875% sales tax plus your local tax if applicable.)

Sales Tax: _______

Total: __________

Shipping Address: ____________________
____
____

Please make check or money order
payable to: Peaceful Moments, LLC
PO Box 551
Sauk Rapids, MN 56379

Please allow 4 – 6 weeks for delivery.

Peaceful Moments, LLC (320)393-TIME
(8463)
Email: peaceful-moments@hotmail.com
www.PeacefulMomentsLLC.com